Murray, Julie, 1969-
Animals of the rain forest /
[2023].
33305257082903
ca   02/06/24

Rain Forest Life

Animals of the Rain Forest

by Julie Murray

Dash!
LEVELED READERS
An Imprint of Abdo Zoom • abdobooks.com

Dash!
LEVELED READERS

2

Level 1 – Beginning
Short and simple sentences with familiar words or patterns for children who are beginning to understand how letters and sounds go together.

Level 2 – Emerging
Longer words and sentences with more complex language patterns for readers who are practicing common words and letter sounds.

Level 3 – Transitional
More developed language and vocabulary for readers who are becoming more independent.

THIS BOOK CONTAINS
RECYCLED MATERIALS

abdobooks.com

Published by Abdo Zoom, a division of ABDO, PO Box 398166, Minneapolis, Minnesota 55439.
Copyright © 2023 by Abdo Consulting Group, Inc. International copyrights reserved in all countries.
No part of this book may be reproduced in any form without written permission from the publisher.
Dash!™ is a trademark and logo of Abdo Zoom.

Printed in the United States of America, North Mankato, Minnesota.
102022
012023

Photo Credits: Getty Images, Science Source, Shutterstock
Production Contributors: Kenny Abdo, Jennie Forsberg, Grace Hansen, John Hansen
Design Contributors: Candice Keimig, Neil Klinepier

Library of Congress Control Number: 2022937228

Publisher's Cataloging in Publication Data

Names: Murray, Julie, author.
Title: Animals of the rain forest / by Julie Murray
Description: Minneapolis, Minnesota : Abdo Zoom, 2023 | Series: Rain forest life | Includes online
    resources and index.
Identifiers: ISBN 9781098280086 (lib. bdg.) | ISBN 9781098280611 (ebook) | ISBN 9781098280918
    (Read-to-Me ebook)
Subjects: LCSH: Rain forest animals--Juvenile literature. | Rain forests--Juvenile literature. | Rain forest
    animals--Behavior--Juvenile literature. | Temperate rain forest ecology--Juvenile literature. |
    Zoology--Juvenile literature.
Classification: DDC 577.34--dc23

Table of Contents

Animals of the Rain Forest

Rain forests are an important part of the Earth. They are home to more than half of the world's animals!

Many kinds of mammals live in rain forests. Sloths move slowly in the trees.

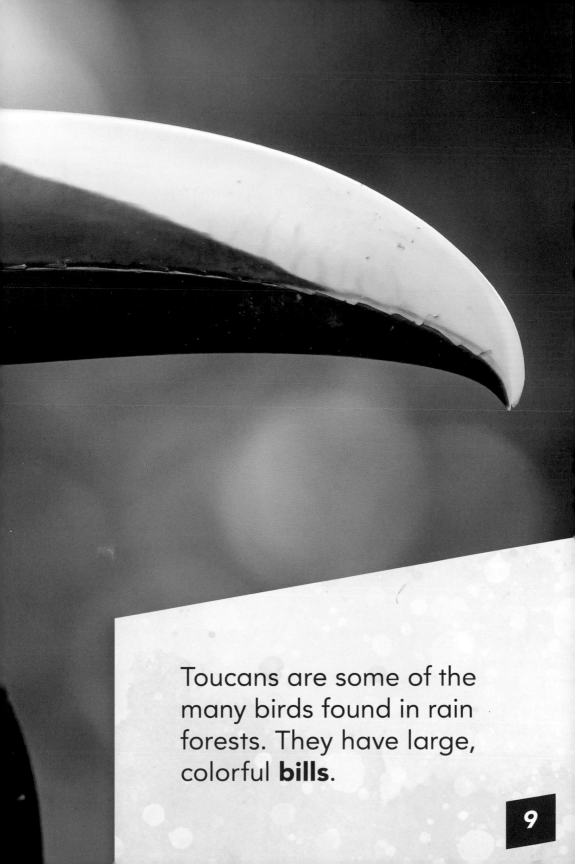

Toucans are some of the many birds found in rain forests. They have large, colorful **bills**.

Around 25% of the world's insect **species** live in rain forests. Elephant beetles can grow more than 4 inches (10 cm) long!

Thousands of different kinds of moths and butterflies fly from plant to plant. The blue morpho butterfly has bright blue wings.

Praying mantises look **delicate**, but they are **fierce** hunters!

15

More than 1,000 kinds of frogs live in rain forests. Poison dart frogs have bright colors. This warns **predators** not to eat them.

Rain forests are home to reptiles too. Many chameleon **species** live in **Madagascar**. Parson's chameleon is the largest.

Green anaconda

Green tree python

Rain forests are good homes for big snakes. Green tree pythons can be found up in trees. Giant green anacondas move easier in water.

More Facts

- Some rain forest animals only live in the trees. They never touch the ground!

- Scientists think there are thousands of undiscovered rain forest animal **species**.

- Hundreds of animal species that live in the rain forests are **endangered**. Deforestation is the main cause. **Climate change** also impacts animal populations.

Glossary

bill – the parts of a bird's jaw that form the beak.

climate change – a change in the usual global and regional climate patterns.

delicate – easy to break or hurt.

endangered – in danger of becoming extinct.

fierce – extremely intense.

Madagascar – an island country in the Indian Ocean off the coast of southern Africa. It is home to some of the world's most unique plants and animals.

predator – an animal that hunts other animals for food.

species – a group of living things that look alike and can have young with one another.

Index

Online Resources

Booklinks
NONFICTION NETWORK
FREE! ONLINE NONFICTION RESOURCES

To learn more about animals of the rain forest, please visit **abdobooklinks.com** or scan this QR code. These links are routinely monitored and updated to provide the most current information available.